CW00349021

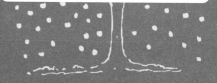

COUNTRY lover

Ed Foster

summersdale

COUNTRY LOVER

Illustrations by Kath Walker

Summersdale Publishers Ltd
46 West Street
Chichester
West Sussex
PO19 1RP
UK

www.summersdale.com

Printed and bound in China

ISBN: 978-1-84953-123-8

Substantial discounts on bulk quantities of Summersdale books are available to corporations, professional associations and other organisations. For details contact Summersdale Publishers by telephone: +44 (0) 1243 771107, fax: +44 (0) 1243 786300 or email: nicky@summersdale.com.

To: ....

From: ....

The country is a place where you have
nothing to do and all day to do it.

John D. Sheridan

'And now here are the results of the sheepdog trails. All the sheepdogs were found not guilty.'

Keith Waterhouse

Great things are done when men and
mountains meet. This is not done
by jostling in the street.

William Blake

A 'tippling cane' is a type of walking stick with a small flask concealed inside. Just the thing for discreetly taking a snifter of something warming on a country walk!

The cowslip is a country wench,

The violet is a nun;

But I will woo the dainty rose,

The queen of every one.

Thomas Hood, 'Flowers'

Nothing is more beautiful than the
loveliness of the woods before sunrise.

George Washington Carver

The English countryside is scoops
of mint ice cream with chips
of chocolate cows.

Jim Bishop

The birch tree symbolises good luck, protection and fertility in English folklore. Until the nineteenth century, a couple who jumped over a birch branch in the doorway of their house could be declared legally wed!

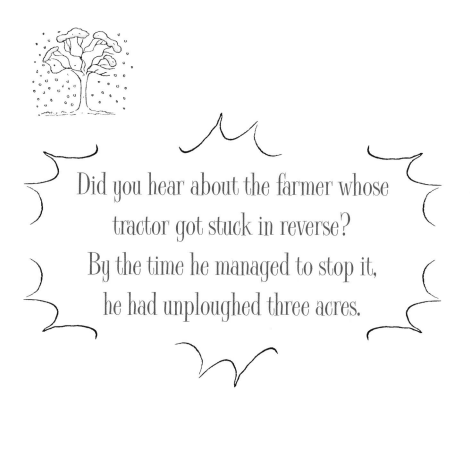

Did you hear about the farmer whose
tractor got stuck in reverse?
By the time he managed to stop it,
he had unploughed three acres.

A horse is a beautiful animal...
it moves as if it always hears music.

Mark Helprin

The cheerful blue cornflower takes its name
from the fields in which it once grew like a
weed. Known in folklore as the Bachelor's
Button, it was once worn by courting young
men. If a flower faded quickly, this indicated
that a man's sweetheart did not
return his affection.

If the rain spoils our picnic, but saves
a farmer's crop, who are we
to say it shouldn't rain?

Tom Barrett

Flowers are the sweetest things God
ever made and forgot to put a soul into.

Henry Ward Beecher

The Cerne Abbas Giant,
a 55-metre-high chalk figure in Dorset,
is believed by some to promote fertility,
especially if a couple have sex lying on his erect
phallus. And maybe there's some truth behind
the myth: women in the surrounding towns
and villages have the highest
birth rate in the UK!

If a pig loses its voice,
is it disgruntled?

Huw Jarsz

To avoid your picnic being ruined by ants try
bringing along some talcum power and putting
a ring around the space you are in. Ants' senses
react with the powder and so they
won't cross over it.

In every walk with nature one receives
far more than he seeks.

John Muir

The farmer allows walkers across the field for free, but the bull charges.

Sign on Irish gate

There was an old man with a beard
Who said, 'It is just as I feared!
Two owls and a hen,
Four larks and a wren,
Have all built their nest in my beard.'

Edward Lear

Anybody can be good in the country.

Oscar Wilde, The Picture of Dorian Gray

In Scotland, it is illegal to be drunk in possession of a cow. The Licensing Act of 1872 explains that operating a horse, cow or steam engine while intoxicated carries a prison sentence or a £200 fine.

God made the country,
and man made the town.

William Cowper, *The Task*

A good farmer is nothing more
nor less than a handy man
with a sense of humus.

Elwyn Brooks White

Deadly nightshade, found in southern and eastern England, is thought to have gained its alternative name, belladonna (from the Italian for 'beautiful lady'), because its juice dilates the pupils of the eye. However, it's a risky route to beauty, as the plant is highly poisonous.

It's spring in England. I missed it
last year. I was in the bathroom.

Michael Flanders

Haggis hurling is a sport similar to many other throwing competitions, except for the added complication that you have to make sure the haggis is still in an edible state when it lands, or you will face disqualification.

Nature is amazing. Who would have
thought of growing a fly swatter
on the rear end of a cow?

Hal Roach

What do you call someone who was once really interested in tractors?
An extractor fan!

A hen is only an egg's way
of making other eggs.

Samuel Butler, *Life and Habit*

Deer antlers are the fastest growing living tissue on earth. They grow from spring to autumn each year, covered in a layer of soft tissue known as 'velvet'. In autumn the velvet falls away and the antlers harden; then in winter they are shed completely, ready for the cycle to begin again the following year.

If you're in the country, take nothing
but pictures, leave nothing but
footprints, kill nothing but time.

Hunter Davies

The tree which moves some to tears of joy is in the eyes of others only a green thing that stands in the way.

William Blake

The average cow produces around 200,000
glasses of milk in its lifetime.

An American man was driving through the English countryside and stopped to ask a farmer for directions. 'Hey, can you tell me the quickest way to get to London?' he asked.

'You drivin' or walkin'?' asked the farmer.

'Driving,' he replied.

The farmer nodded sagely and said, 'Aye, that's certainly the quickest way.'

I'm weary of the endless kerfuffle over fox hunting. I'm told there's a technical term for my condition: tallyhosis.

P. D. Clarke

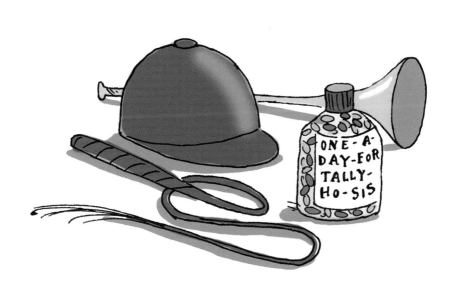

The adder (*Vipera berus*) is Britain's only venomous snake, but luckily adders prefer to stay out of the way when humans approach, and only about ten people have died from their bites in the last hundred years. Strangely, newborn adders often don't eat anything until they are over a year old as they go into hibernation soon after their birth.

You ask of my companions. Hills, sir,
and the sundown, and a dog as large as
myself that my father bought me.

Emily Dickinson

Walking is man's best medicine.

Hippocrates

There'll always be an England
While there's a country lane,
Wherever there's a cottage small
Beside a field of grain.

Ross Parker, 'There'll always be an England'

Rivers know this: there is no hurry.
We shall get there one day.

A. A. Milne, *Winnie the Pooh*

The grey heron, found across Britain and Ireland, has long been associated with bad news and bad luck. Nowadays this is chiefly felt by garden-owners whose fishponds are regularly raided by these keen fishers.

My favourite weather
is bird-chirping weather.

Terri Guillemets

Because of its bright red colour and scent, the fly agaric mushroom was once used as a fly trap. Flies were attracted to the mushroom, licked it and died. Through the centuries, humans have used it for its hallucinogenic properties, though they have to be careful not to go the same way as the flies!

Rain is one thing the British do
better than anybody else.

Marilyn French

A horse is dangerous at both ends and
uncomfortable in the middle.

Ian Fleming

Fortunate too is the man who has come
to know the gods of the countryside.

Virgil, *Georgics*

A woodpecker's tongue is five times as long as its beak. From its anchor near the bird's right nostril, it curls around the skull and down the back of the head before finally making its way out through the beak.

Buttercups and daisies,
Oh, the pretty flowers;
Coming ere the Springtime,
To tell of sunny hours.

Mary Howitt, 'Buttercups and Daisies'

Farmer Smith won the top farming prize this year for being outstanding in his field.

An ancient class struggle can be found in the names we give our animals. When the Normans conquered England in 1066, they used their own Old French words *boef* and *moton* for the beef and mutton on their tables. The Saxon herdsmen who tended their new overlords' animals continued to use their Old English words, which survive today as 'cow' and 'sheep'.

A light wind swept over the corn, and
all nature laughed in the sunshine.

Anne Brontë, *The Tenant of Wildfell Hall*

Noise proves nothing. Often a hen who has merely laid an egg cackles as if she had laid an asteroid.

Mark Twain

The pollen grains from a forget-me-not are
so small that you could fit 10,000
on the head of a pin!

Why do cows wear bells
around their necks?
Because their horns don't work.

A dog is one of the remaining reasons
why some people can be persuaded
to go for a walk.

O. A. Battista

And hear the pleasant cuckoo,
loud and long –
The simple bird that thinks
two notes a song.

W. H. Davies, 'April's Charms'

It's not just humans who like to make their homes smell fresh: female blue tits often weave aromatic plants like lavender and mint into their nests to keep them clean. Starlings also collect nice-smelling plants as part of their courtship rituals.

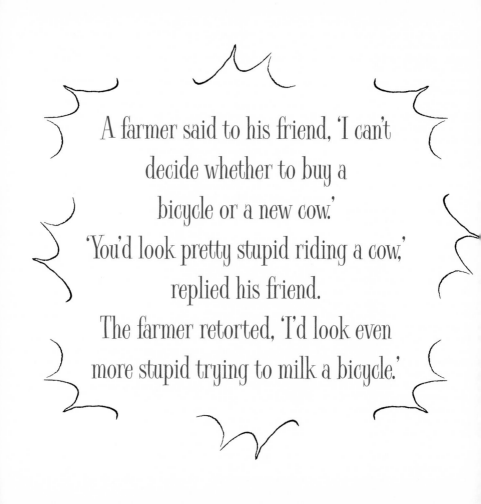

A farmer said to his friend, 'I can't decide whether to buy a bicycle or a new cow.'
'You'd look pretty stupid riding a cow,' replied his friend.
The farmer retorted, 'I'd look even more stupid trying to milk a bicycle.'

To learn something new, take the
path that you took yesterday.

John Burroughs

Come live with me and be my Love,
And we will all the pleasures prove
That hills and valleys, dale and field,
And all the craggy mountains yield.

Christopher Marlowe, 'The Passionate Shepherd to his Love'

Dowsing is an ancient method of searching for
anything that is otherwise hidden, using a pair
of metal rods, a wand or a pendulum. Although
dowsing is often associated with detecting
underground water courses, the method can
be used to locate anything. It is even used
sometimes to detect diseases
in plants and animals.

What do you call a three-legged donkey?
A wonkey.

I am fond of pigs.

Dogs look up to us.

Cats look down on us.

Pigs treat us as equal.

Winston Churchill

Before the advent of high street pharmacies, country dwellers found cures for their ills in the plants that grew around them. For example, dandelion juice has been used to remove warts, ivy leaves to treat corns, and even today we still use dock leaves to calm nettle stings.

It is pleasant to have been to a
place the way a river went.

Henry David Thoreau

Two dogs meet in the park one day. One of them says to the other, 'Woof ! '
The other replies, 'Moo!'
The first dog is perplexed. 'Moo?
Why did you say moo?'
The other dog explains, 'I'm trying to learn a foreign language.'

Morey Amsterdam

If you see a bull while wearing a red jacket,
don't be scared: bulls are actually colour-blind.
They're attracted to movement, rather than
colour, so if a bull charges at you it is a good
idea to throw something like a jacket away
from yourself. The bull should be distracted
by the movement and chase the object instead.
Hopefully.

I had rather be on my farm than
be emperor of the world.

George Washington

There is no season such delight can bring

As summer, autumn, winter and the spring.

William Browne, 'Variety'

Earth and sky, woods and fields, lakes and rivers, the mountain and the sea, are excellent schoolmasters, and teach some of us more than we can ever learn from books.

John Lubbock

May the countryside and the gliding
valley streams content me. Lost to fame,
let me love river and woodland.

Virgil, *Eclogues*

www.summersdale.com